CW01668216

CONTENTS

The Fireside Book

A picture and a poem
for every mood
chosen by

David Hope

Printed and published by
D.C. THOMSON & CO., LTD.,
185 Fleet Street, LONDON EC4A 2HS.
© D.C. Thomson & Co., Ltd., 1993
ISBN 0-85116-569-9

DAWN

DAWN — and a cloudless sky
With a brisk breeze blowing;
And the seabirds' flight
In the morning light,
As the waves go racing by
With their white crests showing.

Dawn of a new-born day,
With the chill night dying
As the shadows flee
To windward and lee,
And the sharp prow cleaves the spray,
At the forefoot flying.

Dawn o'er the ocean dim
With the big sails shaking;
And the long white wake
Where the foam flecks break,
And Nature singing a hymn
To the glad day waking.

Dawn of a radiant day
Bright with the hope of homing,
As each sailor boy
With a heart of joy,
Singing his glad roundelay,
Returns from his roaming.

C.W. Wade

PRIMITIVE MAN

HE lived in a cave by the seas,
He lived upon oysters and foes,
But his list of forbidden degrees,
An extensive morality shows;
Geological evidence goes
To prove he had never a pan,
But he shaved with a shell when he chose —
'Twas the manner of Primitive Man.

He worshipp'd the rain and the breeze,
He worshipp'd the river that flows,
And the dawn, and the moon, and the trees,
And bogles, and serpents, and crows;
He buried his dead with their toes
Tucked-up, an original plan,
Till their knees came right under their nose —
'Twas the manner of Primitive Man.

His communal wives, at his ease,
He would curb with occasional blows;
Or his State had a queen, like the bees
(As another philosopher trows).
When he spoke, it was never in prose,
But he sang in a strain that would scan,
For (to doubt it, perchance, were morose)
'Twas the manner of Primitive Man!

On the coasts that incessantly freeze,
With his stones, and his bones, and his bows,
On luxuriant tropical leas,
Where the Summer eternally glows,
He is found, and his habits disclose
(Let theology say what she can)
That he lived in the long, long agos,
'Twas the manner of Primitive Man!

Andrew Lang

THE FOUR SEASONS ON A FARM

WHEN the days are growing shorter and the nights are getting long,
And there comes a sort of sadness in the robin's evening song.
A feeling of contentment settles down upon us all,
For our busy days are over when the leaves begin to fall.

When the hay is in the haggard, and the corn is in the barn,
And the women start their knitting rolling balls of fleecy yarn,
There's a coolness in the shadows as they lie along the wall,
And we're glad the turf is ready when the leaves begin to fall.

The cows come home to milking as if glad to know a
roof,
And the horses take it easy putting down a slower
hoof;
There's bedding in the stable and there's fodder in
the stall,
As the days approach their shortest here in County
Donegal.

The springtime brings us beauty, but it brings hard
labour, too;
What with ploughing and with seeding and a
hundred jobs to do;
And in Summertime a body has no chance for rest
at all,
Till September days are over and the leaves begin
to fall.

Oh! Then a home is pleasant with folk so good
and kind,
The plough and harrow idle, and the harvest off
our mind;
With potatoes picked and pitted, from the big ones
to the small,
Sure a man may well be happy here in peaceful
Donegal.

Anonymous

THE SAGES

IN our small town you often meet
Professors walking in the street;
They slowly move in grave black gown,
Their eyes are always looking down,
Their brows are furrowed up in thought
As though for some great truth they sought,
With spectacles before their eyes
They look, I must say, very wise.
It seems a pity, now and then
That they don't smile, these learned men.
But as they pass, they don't see me,
Nor yet the birds upon the tree,
Nor the blue sky, nor sun, nor flowers,
Nor any beauty, but for hours
Their chins upon their chests bend they,
And full of wisdom wend their way.

Mabel V. Irvine

SPRING SONG

SOFT pussy-willow bids a glad "Good Morning"
To the river, as it chuckles, rushing by.
The farm dog greets his master, stretching, yawning,
And wild geese, in formation, cross the sky.

Bright daffodils are laughing in the sunshine,
And flirting with the breeze among the leaves,
While from the farm, smoke rises in a blue line,
And gentle doves are cooing in the eaves.

Grey mother-sheep call out an urgent warning
To their straying lambs who answer, cry for cry.
The earth sings out her Spring song to the morning,
And man and bird and beast all make reply.

Iris Hesselden

THE DRAWING-ROOM CLOCK

I LOVE the golden clock that stands
On Mummy's mantel-shelf.
All round the little sky-blue hours
Are wreaths of pink and purple flowers,
I think it likes itself.

I often watch its silver hands
Creep slowly round its face,
And all the time it seems to say,
"Tick-tick, tick-tick, this happy day
Has made my minutes race."

I always think its minute hand
Moves very, very slow,
And yet the really-truly time
Goes very quick whenever I'm
Playing down here, I know.

I think that's why that little clock
Has such a happy look;
It knows how much I love to be
Comfy upon my Mummy's knee,
With some dear story book.

And when at last I must to bed,
Its friendly, silvery ticks
Call down to me, "Good-night, good-night,
Tomorrow will be just as bright.
I'm sorry to strike six!"

Mabel V. Irvine

SIMPLE THINGS

ARE these, the simple, common things,
The source from which true beauty springs?

The early bird that hops at dawn
To catch the worms upon the lawn;

The bright-hued rainbow's arching span,
Beyond the range of mortal man;

The barley swelling, heads bowed down,
A rippling sea of golden brown;

Shrill seagulls and the breakers' roar
Along the runnelled, sandy shore;

Green treetops swaying in the breeze,
While in their shade cows stand, at ease;

The brooks that croon their soothing tales
To restless rivers in the vales;

Like a mirror, the silver pool
Reflecting children home from school;

The red sun dipping in the west,
The falling dusk, and time for rest.

The source from which true beauty springs
Lies in the simple, common things.

Glynfab John

IRISH JIG

I MET one day a mountain man,
A mountain man,
A mountain man,
I met one day a mountain man
Not far from green Killarney.
He sang a song and he played a tune,
A wayward, winsome, wooing croon,
And said I was fresh as a rose in June,
But that was only his blarney.

He danced me round in the grey twilight,
The grey twilight,
The grey twilight,
He danced me round in the grey twilight
On the Pins of Connemara.
With a jig and a twirl and twist and hop,
He danced me over each high hill top,
We danced until I was like to drop,
From Donegal Bay to Tara.

We swirled like dust until break of dawn,
The break of dawn,
The break of dawn,
We swirled like dust until break of dawn,
Then he gave me a silver penny.
He kissed my lips and he pressed my hand,
Then left me alone on the coral strand,
For he was away to fairyland
In the magical moss of Kilkenny.

M. L. Dalgleish

PARIS IN SPRING

THE city's all a-shining
  Beneath a fickle sun,
A gay young wind's a-blowing,
  The little shower is done.
But the rain-drops still are clinging
  And falling one by one —
Oh, it's Paris, it's Paris,
  And Springtime has begun!

I know the Bois is twinkling
  In a sort of hazy sheen,
And down the Champs the grey old arch
  Stands cold and still between.
But the walk is flecked with sunlight
  Where the great acacias lean,
Oh, it's Paris, it's Paris,
  And the leaves are growing green.

The sun's gone in, the sparkle's dead,
  There falls a dash of rain,
But who would care when such an air
  Comes blowing up the Seine?
And still Ninette sits sewing
  Beside her window-pane,
When it's Paris, it's Paris,
  And Springtime's come again!

Sara Teasdale

THE PROBLEM

IF all my love were little stars
    They'd form a galaxy;
And should they change to raindrops
    They would overflow the sea.

If all my love were music
    You would hear a minuet;
And if it changed to waltz-time
    We might well be dancing yet.

If all my love were feathers
    They would flight a million birds;
But now your hand is holding mine
    I'm at a loss for words!

Peter Cliffe

AN AUNT'S APOLOGY

SERENA! most patient of nieces,
You'll think I've forgotten to make
A frock for your doll from those pieces
Of muslin I tore for your sake.
But things that are best ripen slowly,
And Rome was not built in a day,
So I trust, dear, my work will now wholly
Make up for each tedious delay.
Every stitch of the frock I am sending
I worked at by mornings and eves,
'Twas I did the darning and mending,
'Twas I made those sweet little sleeves.
And if I've done some of it badly,
And put in my stitches aslant,
Just say, when you glance at it sadly,
"'Twas made by my well-meaning Aunt."
The flounce dolly's frock now adorning
I wore on my own at fifteen,
Ah! that was in life's early morning,
Don't count up the years flown between.
Old friends are the best — so I felt, dear,
And of all I am sending to you,
You'll find nothing new but the belt, dear,
And streamers of Mexican blue.
Paler tints in *my* day were the fashion,
Very faint were *my* ribbons of blue,
Yet proudly I fastened the sash on
That marked me as loyal and true!
Yes! believe me the old friend's the dearest,
Old picture, old book, or old chaunt,
And of old friends the truest and queerest,
Pray count your affectionate Aunt.

Anon.

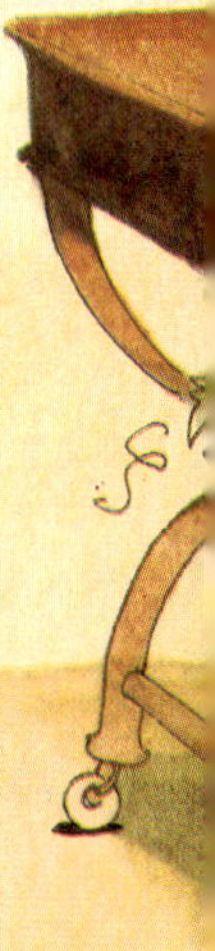

THE LONELY FARING

O MY dear, my dear!
If we were talking.
If we were walking
The old, old ways by the Wizard Stone!
But it's one comes only;
'Tis I go lonely,
Walking and talking with myself alone.

O my dear, my dear!
I see with your eyes,
I hear as it flies,
Your song go round by the old hearth stone;
But you never come
By loch or river;
Far out I am faring alone, alone.

Jessie Mackay

THE VAMP

IN spite of homely features
Or asymmetric form,
The plainest of God's creatures
Can take men's hearts by storm
If she possesses charm and wit
And that appeal which folks call "It".

An aunt of mine, Aunt Gladys,
Provides a case in point;
She leaves much lovelier ladies
With noses out of joint,
For though exceptionally plain
She seldom yet has lacked a swain.

She never wearies telling
Of how her charm allures,
And of her plans for quelling
Men's am'rous overtures.
Her efforts meet, one must confess,
With quite unqualified success.

For though her lovers scheme to
Desert their lawful wives,
And sometimes even dream, too,
Of leading double lives,
They never go too far, poor chaps,
Or even far enough, perhaps.

All men are mad about her
(At least, she tells me so);
They cannot live without her,
And though some do, I know,
The others, when she turns them down,
Will shoot themselves, or else
leave town.

Thus, all through her existence,
She strives, with subtle arts,
To keep men at a distance
And yet to win their hearts,
And so, by simple strength of will,
My aunt remains a spinster still.

Harry Graham

THE SKYLARK

THE grove's green trees to other birds,
  To thee the sky is given;
They warble sweet in earthly words,
Thou speak'st the tongue of heaven:
Bird of the quivering wing and silver song,
Whose trembling heart of joy
Showers o'er the world
Honeyed contentment from unclouded skies;
To thee the far and fathomless depths belong,
Where thy voice faints and dies!
While other songsters cease to sing
When their fond matings end,
Thou singest on, and oft to Winter's sun
A welcome thou dost bring;
Each season is thy friend,
And thou forgettest none.

John Hogben

B. Glebska

ON ARRAN

YELLOW of gorse and purple of heather,
Glint of the sun on the upland track,
Feathery clouds and halcyon weather —
Hasten your steps and take up your pack!

Blue of the sky and brown of the river,
Gleam of the light on the rippling burn,
Ribbon of green where the rushes quiver,
Dappled shade at the road's turn.

Take the rough track — lift your face to the mountain,
Climb to the heights of the lonely bens.
Follow the grouse and walk with the eagle,
See, far beneath, the green of the glens.

Amber of lochans and blackness of peat hags —
White of the smoke on the evening air.
A song on your lips and joy in your footstep,
Gold shines the sunlight and gone is dull care.

Down by the slipway, asleep in the noontide,
Cottages lie in the Summer calm.
Sweet is the scent of myrtle and heather,
And after the rain the cool air is balm.

This then, the scene of Arran in Summer —
Isle of the high tops, jewel of the West.
Where'er I roam throughout all my lifetime,
Isle of my heart, thou art dearest and best.

Frances Reed

WINE

THE connoisseur may laud liqueur
 (As made by monks in cloisters)
Or rave about the velvet stout
 That's used to wash down oysters;
Such drinks are not for me or mine,
 The only drink I need is WINE!

Though brandy may, so people say,
 Be termed the drink for heroes,
And for one's aunt a Crême de Menthe
 Seems popular at Ciro's,
At peppermint I draw the line,
 The nectar of the Gods was WINE!

The old sea-dog must have his grog
 When on the briny ocean,
And dukes on yachts use rum in tots
 As a laryngean lotion;
But when I sail across the brine
 I never touch a thing but WINE.

Yes, give me port (the vintage sort),
 Champagne and hock and claret
And e'en moselle, and I shall dwell
 Contented in a garret.
In exile I would never pine
 If I were well supplied with WINE.

So let's combine before its shrine
 To sin with vinous unction,
Ere we recline upon the spine,
 And wits decline to function,
While still, in fine, we can design
 Some eight or nine new rhymes to WINE!

Harry Graham

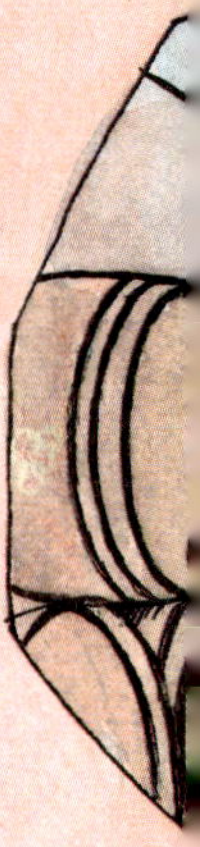

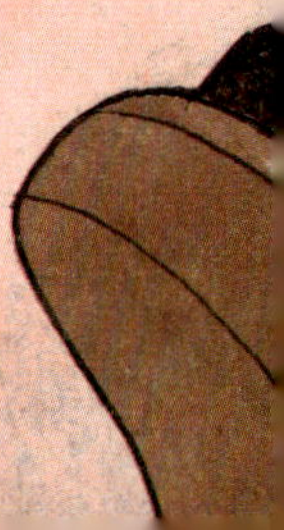

BACCHUS

BABY-GIRL

THE baby-girl next door is such a restless little sprite,
She never gives us any peace from morning until night;
She's always running up the path and climbing through our fence,
And peeping in our washhouse door — the little Impudence!

She picks our flowers and scares our cat, and every afternoon,
When Dad and I take forty winks, she sings a lusty tune;
Or she drags her little go-cart up and down the yard with glee,
Till there's not a thought of sleep for Dad and not a wink for me.

She puts stones in our water-can with manner like a queen's!
She pulls the scarlet blossoms off our cherished kidney beans.
There's not a seed-patch anywhere without her footmarks showing;
She's always "dest a-comin' " or else she's "dest a-goin' "!

A tiresome little child? I beg your pardon, Mrs Brown:
There's not another such a bairn lives in or out this town!
I'll thank you to be careful, Ma'am! A nuisance? That she's not!
She's the dearest — and the only — little grandchild that we've got!

Fay Inchfawn

FROM THE TOWPATH

SLOWLY moving through the water,
Gently chugging on her way,
Comes the narrow boat a-dawdling
Through the warm September day.
Wavelets lap among the rushes
Slapping softly on her sides,
Ducks and moorhens bob behind her
In the back-wash as she glides.
On her cabin, painted ribbons
Intertwine each scarlet rose
Gleaming brass and shining windows
In reflection as she goes.
Nosing now beneath the willows,
Disappearing down the stream,
Hidden half in trembling shadows
Vanished silent as a dream.

Margaret Ingall

ROSE

SONNET

HIS wanderings over, home Odysseus came,
Unrecognised alike by friend and foe;
But as he reached the lofty portico
Where Argus lay in misery and shame —
Aged and toothless, blind, diseased, and lame —
The old hound knew his lord of long ago,
Raised his grey head his faithful love to show;
Then joy and death swept through him like a flame.

My Hamish, when you go as go you must,
Some day, like Argus, down the shadowy trail
That leads both dogs and men to quiet dust,
Surely your eager spirit will prevail;
Ears pricked, eyes bright in gaiety and trust,
You'll greet dark Charon with a wagging tail.

M. L. Dalgleish

THE MANSE GARDEN

THE garden was something to see
And my father attended it well.
Even now I remember the spell
And the freshness of flower, fruit and tree.

There our ebony cat would run free,
Or purr in her green citadel.
The garden was something to see
And my father attended it well.

Mind-pictures of bean, lettuce, pea —
The bright berries — the apples that fell —
Revolve in a slow carousel.

Lupins, roses, and poppies! For me,
The garden was something to see!
And my father attended it well.

May C. Jenkins

THE WOOER

I'LL sing thee songs of Araby,
And tales of fair Kashmir,
Wild tales to cheat thee of a sigh,
Or charm thee to a tear.
And dreams of delight shall on thee break,
And rainbow visions rise,
And all my soul shall strive to wake
Sweet wonder in thine eyes.

Through those twin lakes, when wonder wakes,
My raptured song shall sink,
And as the diver dives for pearls,
Bring bright tears to their brink;
And dreams of delight shall on thee break
And rainbow visions rise,
And all my soul shall strive to wake
Sweet wonder in thine eyes.

W. G. Wills

Love Songs
Love Songs

IMAGES

THE images I have in mind
Are of the most enduring kind:

Pink blossom on the cherry-trees,
Like candy-floss licked by the breeze;

The dingle where the bluebells mass
Amid the green of fern and grass;

The brook that babbles on downhill
While sheep and cattle drink their fill;

The cascades from a waterfall
That spray with mist the garden wall;

Skylarks at dizzy heights that spill
Their hymns upon God's window-sill;

Leaves in the Autumn drifting down
With hues of yellow, red and brown;

The whiteness of the first fresh snow
Cleansing the sullied earth below;

Stars shooting through the frosty night
With all too quickly burnt-out light;

The images I have in mind
I still would see if I were blind.

Glynfab John

SUMMER

WHEN days are warm and golden-lazy,
Bright with buttercup and daisy,
Rich in swallows, flying over,
Busy bees among the clover.
When favourite haunts and secret ways
Are fragrant with pink dog-rose sprays,
And river banks sport waving sedge,
Comfrey, flag and hawthorn hedge . . .
That's the time for boating trips,
Ploughman's fare and cider-sips,
Evening strolls and rosy dawns,
And strawberry teas on Summer lawns.

Fiona Walker

DOG
AND
FOX

A WISH

FROM this city balcony,
    Would that through those rustling trees
Instead of concrete, there could be
A glimpse of blue, exotic sea!

A trail of silver sand which wound
From the gloomy closemouth, bound
On a rustling, secret way
Through the trees down to the bay;

Bougainvillaea, scented hot,
Wreathed about my tubs and pots,
Humming birds with plumage rare
Perched upon my easy chair.

Drawn by the ocean's timeless roar
I'd rush from pavement grey to shore,
And there, by wind and spray caressed,
I'd sing and shout for joyfulness!

Eileen Melrose

THE TIRED WOMAN'S EPITAPH

HERE lies a poor woman, who always was tired;
She lived in a house where help was not hired.
Her last words on earth were: "Dear friends, I am going
Where washing ain't done, nor sweeping, nor sewing;
But everything there is exact to my wishes,
For where they don't eat there's no washing of dishes.
I'll be where loud anthems will always be ringing,
But, having no voice, I'll be clear of the singing.
Don't mourn for me now; don't mourn for me never—
I'm going to do nothing for ever and ever . . ."

Anon.

Here lies...

GOOD COMPANION

WHEN on my way, to rest awhile,
My heavy pack I've downed,
The rucksack nestles at my feet,
As might a faithful hound;
And somehow thus confides to me
(Though uttering no sound)
That through the years together we
Have trekked a deal of ground.

Most frames are made of alloy now,
Much lighter, it is true;
They balance higher on your back
To ease the strain on you;
The fabric's made of nylon tough —
That cuts the weight down, too —
And coloured bright, for safety's sake,
In mountain orange hue.

Should I discard this sober green,
A lurid eyesore buy?
Old leather straps embrace me tight
And tell of friendship's tie.
I'll not betray my comrade staunch,
And here's one reason why . . .
He may be old and overweight,
But so, I fear, am I!

George Darwall

TO THE MANNER BORN

VEXED hub,
Sans club,
Leaves wife,
Home strife;
Stalks off,
Tries golf.

Blythe he!
Makes tee,
Neat, tall,
Tops ball:
Great wax;
More whacks!

Breaks shaft;
Looks daft.
Once more
Cries "Fore!"
Lost ball;
Sings small!

Not done;
New one;
Smites hard—
Bunkered!
Sweats, mopes;
Then slopes!

John Hogben

TIMES OF NEED

THESE times, God bless our Essex grass,
  That it may rich hay-harvest yield:
Bless dairy farm and market plot,
    Garden and hive and furrowed field;
Our fruit from gales, and roots from drought,
    And labouring folk from danger shield.

In Walthams, Easters, Roothings all,
    God grant the weather hold this year
Till the last loads be safely stored,
    The last reaped lands of sheaves be clear;
Till "All ye thankful people, come,"
    On Sunday sung in church we hear!

Arthur Shearly Cripps

THE FOREST

THERE is the sound of music
In every woodland tree,
And sweeter far than pipe or flute
This vibrant melody,
For all the birds are singing,
Their lady loves to woo,
As the first rays of sunlight
Silver the morning dew.

Wild flowers fringe the streamlet
Meandering on its way,
Joining the songbirds' chorus
In gentle harmony;
A squirrel boldly ventures
And scuttles through the sedge,
To trace a cooling pathway
Along the water's edge.

How lovely is the forest!
You ask how long I'd stay?
For ever, in this haven —
Forever and a day!
I'd make a little cabin,
And in the forest find
A life of rich contentment,
And leave the world behind.

Patricia McGavock

ESCAPE

SOON I shall close and lock the door,
Knowing this town has nothing more to give;
Heartsick for clover fields, a cloudy moor,
The old, grey farmhouse where my kinsfolk live.

Belongings packed, I'll simply walk away,
Leaving the burden of a dragging care;
Accepting there is little I can say
To men who find suburban joys more fair

Than mist uprising in a valley cool
As day goes by and one bright star appears.
To you who smile at such a dreaming fool
I answer: I have put an end to tears.

The country heart a dreary prison finds
Where sullen streets endure the traffic's roar.
Give me a sleepy road that gently winds
Onwards to heart's content. I close the door.

Peter Cliffe

NIDDERDALE

TWO things I love in this most lovely dale:
A stream of amber water, clear and chill,
O'er slope stones slipping, or at wayward will
Breaking smooth silence to a silver tale;
A firwood then, fanned by a gentle gale
To lose its scent; within the trunks are still,
And pillar a dark shrine for dreams to fill;
Between the stones the unsunned grass is pale.

Two things I loved; but thou, o lovelier
Than these, hast all that these were worth to me;
Thy clearer eyes know more of change and stir
Than all the brooks, thy tongue more melody;
And 'neath thy shadowy hair, thy serene face
Makes sanctuary in the holy place.

Henry Charles Beeching

WHERE LILIES GROW

SHADY and lone the quiet vale
Where lilies grow;
Gently they sway and gently peal
Their bells of snow.

Not theirs to sound the tocsin dread;
They do but tell
The lime-tree blossoms overhead
They love them well.

And with that small blithe melody a scent
Floats up from earth
To meet a perfume redolent
Of heavenly birth.

Nina Cust

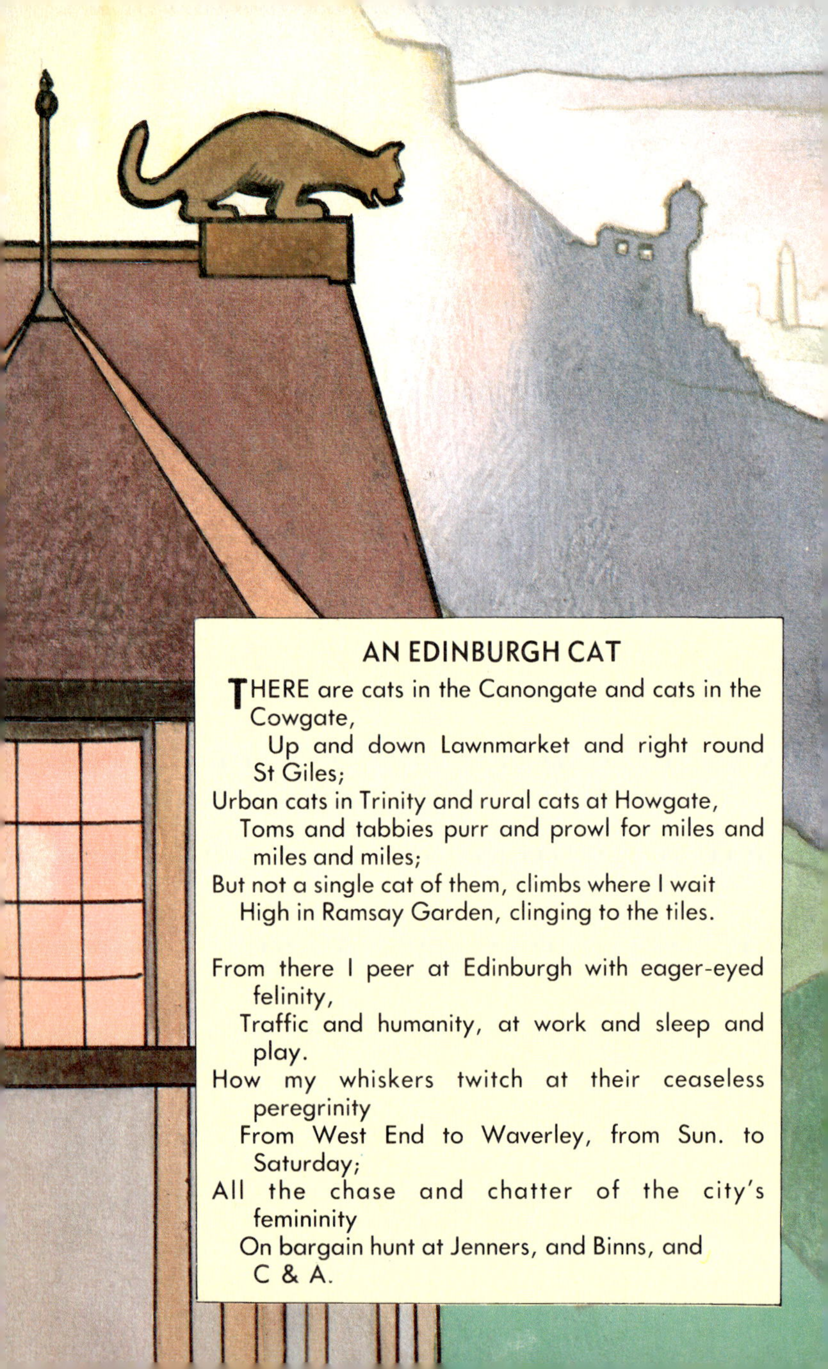

AN EDINBURGH CAT

THERE are cats in the Canongate and cats in the Cowgate,
Up and down Lawnmarket and right round St Giles;
Urban cats in Trinity and rural cats at Howgate,
Toms and tabbies purr and prowl for miles and miles and miles;
But not a single cat of them, climbs where I wait
High in Ramsay Garden, clinging to the tiles.

From there I peer at Edinburgh with eager-eyed felinity,
Traffic and humanity, at work and sleep and play.
How my whiskers twitch at their ceaseless peregrinity
From West End to Waverley, from Sun. to Saturday;
All the chase and chatter of the city's femininity
On bargain hunt at Jenners, and Binns, and C & A.

Storm clouds over Fife; in the Firth the white spray curling;
Loud with the nor-easter, I shriek a merry mew;
Summer time in Princes Street; kilted dancers whirling
Where the flowery gardens hear my purring all night thro'.
Bagpipes on the Esplanade, and high above their skirling,
I sing in shrill cacophony my joy at the Tattoo.

Greyfriars Bobby sits smug beside his Candlemakers,
A burgess and a movie star, grown pompous by renown;
The unicorn of Mercat Cross mounts guard on holy acres,
Law-abiding citizens who view me with a frown;
Yet if ever I fall victim to town planners and house-breakers,
My loss would be catastrophe for Edinburgh town.

Note: The cat of the poem is a carving on the gable of Ramsay Garden beside the Castle Esplanade.

M. L. Dalgleish

WEEDS WELCOME

I KNOW it's not God who decided,
Which flower is labelled a weed,
He only created their petals,
Their colour, their size and their seed.

It hurt me as I pushed the mower,
And chopped off each pretty, white head,
When I'd really prefer Nature's bounty,
Not lawn but a meadow instead.

So now I've dug up all the daisies,
My lawn, it conforms, neat and green,
But I'm keeping a part of the garden,
Where daisies and vetch can be seen.

This wilderness I have named Eden,
For in Paradise God first decreed,
That flowers were meant to be flowers,
Protected, not killed as a weed.

Chrissy Greenslade

SUITORS

THOUGH Alan has such lovely eyes,
He's much too quick to criticise
The way I always do my hair,
The kind of clothes I like to wear.

And Michael is a handsome lad,
But so precise he'd drive me mad.
He gets quite cross if I am late,
And sometimes doesn't even wait.

Henry hopes I'll change my ways
And go for every modern craze;
Tint my hair a vivid green,
Just like a monster on the screen.

But Sam's an understanding boy
Who shares the things that I enjoy.
So I am going to marry Sam,
Who loves me just the way I am!

Peter Cliffe

THE HARRIER PACK

THROUGH woodland and valley the echoes fly
back:
Oh, hark to the cry of our Harrier Pack!
They know how to work and they've plenty of
drive —
The bracken and bramble are fairly alive,
As thrusting and eager, they push him along;
And Wiseman is speaking, he cannot be wrong.
There's Statesman and Harvester chiming away,
And Fancy is cutting the work out to-day,
While Vixen and Freedom are following fast
(I'm glad to see Nimble has entered at last).

Though Witchcraft was throwing a riotous tongue
In covert, she's on with the rest of them flung.
They're crossing the valley! They're racing the hill!
Their hackles are up and they're running to kill.
That fox will have luck if he wins to his earth,
So sit down and gallop for all you are worth!
The country is rough and not easy to ride;
They cross and re-cross to the coomb's farther side.
But, slip along quick or they may not come back:
Hark forrard away, to our Harrier Pack!

Iris M. Raikes

REFLECTIONS

DEEP in the river white clouds sail by,
And brown cows stand in the liquid sky.

Tall tree-trunks taper far down below,
Their green leaves quiver when breezes blow.

Oh, what a strange world here is begun,
Where sky and water merge into one;

Where the swallows skim the river-bed —
Or am I standing upon my head?

Where the fishes swim in cloud-splashed sky
And dodge those swallows fast-skimming by;

Where weeds and pebbles and branches crowd,
And the cattle drink great draughts of cloud;

Where winds shake the trees and make no sound —
But am I alive, or am I drowned?

Glynfab John

LOVE STORY

As Sally Grey walks down our street,
 The church bells all start ringing,
While in a chorus when we meet
 The birds are wildly singing.

Then Sally Grey gives me her hand
 And says she loves me only.
Now I'm the proudest in the land
 Who once was sad and lonely.

Soon Sally Grey will take my name,
 The parson fast shall bind us.
Oh, surely there'll be none to blame
 Who faithful ever find us.

And when our youth has flown away,
 She'll still be as entrancing
As when she was sweet Sally Grey
 Who set my young heart dancing.

Peter Cliffe

BARNEY

SCRAP of white and tan,
Little Barney!
Straight you talked and ran;
Never blarney;
In your Wicklow blood,
You beguiled,
Though you truly stood
Ireland's child!

If a mastiff lay
In your path,
Did you tremble? Nay,
Spite its wrath.
Like a gamesome buck,
Faced you collie —
Some would call it pluck,
Others folly.

Such your will to live,
    Can it be
Right alone to give
    Immortality
To a man, though mean —
    Heaven his goal?
Nay, still fights unseen
    Your intrepid soul!

John Hogben

THE MOORLAND

PLEASANT the ways by vale and stream when
Spring was in the land;
Beech, and oak, and elm-tree boughs — green
boughs on every hand;
Pleasant the song of birds at morn from every
orchard-close,
And the very soul of Summer abloom within the
heart of the rose.

But give me a stretch of gorse and broom, and
heathery moorlands wide,
With staff, and pack, and a light heart, and a
comrade true and tried;
Give me a wind that clears the brain of the dust and
stain of toil,
The wild wind, the moor wind — the breath of
English soil.

Give me a path a man may tread where God is over
all,
And nothing is heard save the wind's song, and the
wailing curlew's call;
With the moorland stretching around — around —
as far as the eye can see,
For that, when the burden is hard to bear, is the
only path for me.

Tinsley Pratt

AUTUMN BABY

MARY FELICITY came to me
When the leaves were golden on every tree,
And her downy head is golden brown
To match the leaves that are drifting down.

Mary Felicity came when the days
Of September were wrapped in a still blue haze,
And when she awakens, her gentle eyes
Are soft and blue like the quiet skies.

Mary Felicity brought with her
A charming smile and a delicate air,
And her warm little mouth is folded close
Like the silken heart of an Autumn rose.

Outside my window a robin's song
Is wistful and sweet the whole day long,
Inside, the least, least cry from you
Is sad and sweet and pierces me through;
May love and tenderness give you rest,
O Mary Felicity, warm on my breast!

Mabel V. Irvine

THE LAST CAST

JUST one cast more! How many a year
   Beside how many a pool and stream,
Beneath the falling leaves and sere,
   I've sighed, reeled up, and dreamed my dream,

Dreamed of the sport since April first
   Her hands fulfilled of flowers and snow,
Adown the pastoral valleys burst
   Where Ettrick and where Teviot flow,

Dreamed of the singing showers that break,
   And sting the lochs, or near or far,
And rouse the trout, and stir the take
   From Urigil to Lochinvar.

Brief are man's days at best; perchance
   I waste my own, who have not seen
The castled palaces of France
   Shine on the Loire in Summer green.

And like a horse unbroken yet,
   The yellow stream with rush and foam,
'Neath tower, and bridge, and parapet,
   Girdles his ancient mistress, Rome!

I may not see them, but I doubt
   If seen I'd find them half so fair
As ripples of the rising trout
   That feed beneath the elms of Yair.

Andrew Lang

THE FUTURE

YOU will never, never catch it,
Though you run with all your might,
For it lies just round the corner,
And 'tis always out of sight.

You think perhaps to reach it
On the summit of the hill,
But fresh heights tower above you,
And you are climbing still.

Even if you go a-sailing,
New countries to explore,
You will scarce discern the outline
Of that undiscovered shore.

'Tis the voice which bids you follow,
'Tis the peak unscaled, supreme,
'Tis the far, and unknown country,
Where you anchored in a dream.

Yet, you hope it lies before you,
That one day you will attain
To a land where all is beauty,
And a world grown young again.

Anne MacDonald

DOG-DAISIES

SKIPPING down the meadow way,
All singing, loud and shrill,
The children picked wild flowers today,
As children always will,
And I, with such unfeigned delight,
Was showered with daisies, gold and white.

Within a cherished ginger-jar,
I've placed each precious one,
So cool, so beautiful they are,
With each small, gleaming sun,
Encircled by a star, so fair,
No other wild flower can compare!

Dog-daisies, fresh as morning dew,
Upon my window-sill,
Every time I look at you
I see the children still,
Bright-eyed and laughing, at the door,
As radiant as the flowers they bore.

Kathleen O'Farrell

BG

A THOUGHT IN THE WOODS

ROUND me the woods lay still,
  Waiting for something and I waited, too.
Could it be Spring? The leaves, already budding,
Whispered that she was there.
Something they waited for —
Waiting, I listened though I knew not why;
It seemed so close, an answer just beginning,
Sighed through the woodland fair.
Listening still, I heard,
Softly the trickling murmur of the brook
Down in the moss, the only sound now stirring
Came from the vale below.
Oh! I could cry aloud!
Something I want, and know not what it is!
What is this thing, this secret you are telling?
Tell me! and let me know.

Iris M. Raikes

A TRAP FOR DREAMS

COME in from the dark night,
  Shut fast the door;
I have kept the lamp alight
  And swept the floor,
And put away from sight
  What passed before.

Be still; rest and forget;
  This hour redeems
The long day's toil and fret;
  The firelight gleams
Where dusk and silence set
  A trap for dreams.

Your tired head resting, so,
  Beneath my hand,
For a little while we'll go
  In twilight land,
Silent, because you know
  I understand.

F. Y. Walters

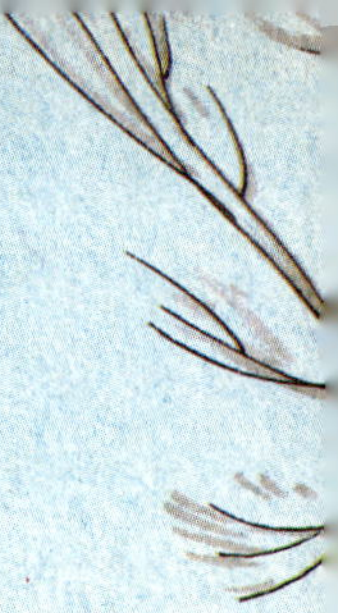

WINTER SUNSHINE

SEE, a shaft of Winter sunlight
  Through the branches slide,
Dappled over leaf and bramble
  Down the woodland ride.

Fields are lying pale and shining
  To the Winter's day,
Hedge and coppice gleaming darkly,
  Still, and far away.

Hounds are driving through the covert,
  Chiming as they pass,
Streaming out across the open
  Stubble-land and grass.

Ever can their magic music
Warm our hearts again,
As the joy of Winter sunshine
After storm and rain.

Iris M. Raikes

SAVING FIRES

THE fire burnt low
   And the load of logs at hand
Dwindled to three — then two — then one.

There was nothing for it when that was done
But to let the fire die out or go
Out through the wind and the brittle snow
To the woodshed behind the house.

Something there is in the heart that rebels
At letting a living flame fall low,
To flicker in fits and starts, then fail
Till the grey ash falls apart, and so
The dark floods in where light had been.

So I pulled up my collar and opened the door.

How many fires I gained that night,
How many fires in saving one!
— Though I felt no need of the hearth's
   poor flame —
For the splendid light of a thousand stars
Lit the torch of each tree, each stone,
Each separate snowflake, and ran along
The smooth ice-surface of path and pool.

And each was fuel for the heart's low fire
Till it smouldered and triumphed with leaping light
And the flickering tongues of awakened song
Threatened the dark and reared to consume
Both the burnt-out ash
And the prowling night.

How many fires
I saved that night!

Lilian Maude Watts

HOMECOMING

THE sun has set against the Winter sky,
The first small stars are shining clear and bright,
And there is peace, as home and friends draw nigh,
The peace that comes with quickly gathering night.

Gone are the small vexations of the day,
Unkindnesses that ruffle mind and will;
It is the true and gentle deeds that stay,
The memory of them lingers with me still.

Gone is the work that put me to the test,
Gone are the crowds — the noisy city's din —
Home is the place, where I am loved the best,
And I feel safe when I set foot therein.

God grant that there may never be a day,
When there is found no longer home for me,
Those sheltering walls, the loyal hearts that stay
Faithful in joy — and in adversity.

Margaret H. Dixon

WIND, SUN AND STARS

FLING the casement wide:
Let the wind blow in,
Fresh from the hills and plains,
The pines, the bracken and whin;
Sweet from over the earth,
Strong from over the sea,
O when the wind sweeps in
It lifts the heart in me!

Fling the windows wide:
Let the sun pour through,
Hot with the blaze of noon,
Fresh with the breath of dew;
Life in his magic touch,
Strength, warmth, ectasy,
O when the sun floods through
It fires the blood in me!

Turn the shutters wide:
Let the stars look down,
Millions of friendly eyes
Watching o'er field and town;
Far in the deep where lie
Wonder, hope, mystery,
Ah, when the stars look down
The soul has peace in me!

Shan Bullock

The artists are:—

Charles Bannerman; The Drawing-Room Clock, Paris In Spring, The Problem, Sonnet, The Wooer, Summer, To The Manner Born, Escape, Suitors, A Trap For Dreams.

Sheila Carmichael; Spring Song, Reflections.

John Dugan; Primitive Man, The Vamp, On Arran, Images, A Wish, Weeds Welcome, The Harrier Pack, Saving Fires.

Colin Gibson; Good Companion, The Last Cast, Dog-Daisies.

Barbara Glebska; Simple Things, The Lonely Faring, The Skylark, Barney, A Thought In The Woods.

Allan Haldane; Dawn, From The Towpath, Where Lilies Grow.

John Mackay; The Sages, Irish Jig, Wine, The Manse Garden, The Tired Woman's Epitaph, Times Of Need, An Edinburgh Cat, The Future, Winter Sunshine, Homecoming.

Sandy Milligan; The Four Seasons On A Farm, The Forest, The Moorland, Wind Sun And Stars.

Staff Artists; An Aunt's Apology, Baby-Girl, Nidderdale, Love Story, Autumn Baby.